MARTA ADT
STARSEEDS MEETING

PUBLISHED BY **ADT & AYALA ART**

MOSCOW, RUSSIA

WWW.ADTAYALA.ART

© 2021 ADT & AYALA ART

ALL RIGHTS RESERVED. NO PORTION OF THIS BOOK MAY BE REPRODUCED
IN ANY FORM WITHOUT PERMISSION FROM THE PUBLISHER:
ADTAYALA@GMAIL.COM

ART AND ILLUSTRATIONS
CREATED FROM ORIGINAL PAINTINGS BY MARTA ADT.
ALL RIGHTS RESERVED.

MADE IN MOSCOW

CONTENTS

DEDICATION vii

MESSAGE TO MY READERS ix

A LITTLE ABOUT ME
Marta Adt's Biography 3

STARSEED AWAKENING
Marta Adt's Spiritual Journey 5

CONNECTED SOULS #2
FEATURED ARTWORK 7

CONNECTED SOULS #2
ART FILM 10

STARSEEDS CHARACTERISTICS
.... 11

MARS&VENUS
FEATURED ARTWORK 15

PLEIADIAN STARSEEDS 17

SIRIAN STARSEEDS 19

ARCTURIAN STARSEEDS 21

LYRAN STARSEEDS 23

VEGA STARSEEDS 25

ORION STARSEEDS 27

MY ASTRAL TRAVEL SESSIONS 31

PERSONAL EXPERIENCES 33

TONAL/NAGUAL
FEATURED ARTWORK 39

FINAL WORDS
.... 41

SPECIAL THANKS
.... 43

CONTACT INFORMATION
.... 44

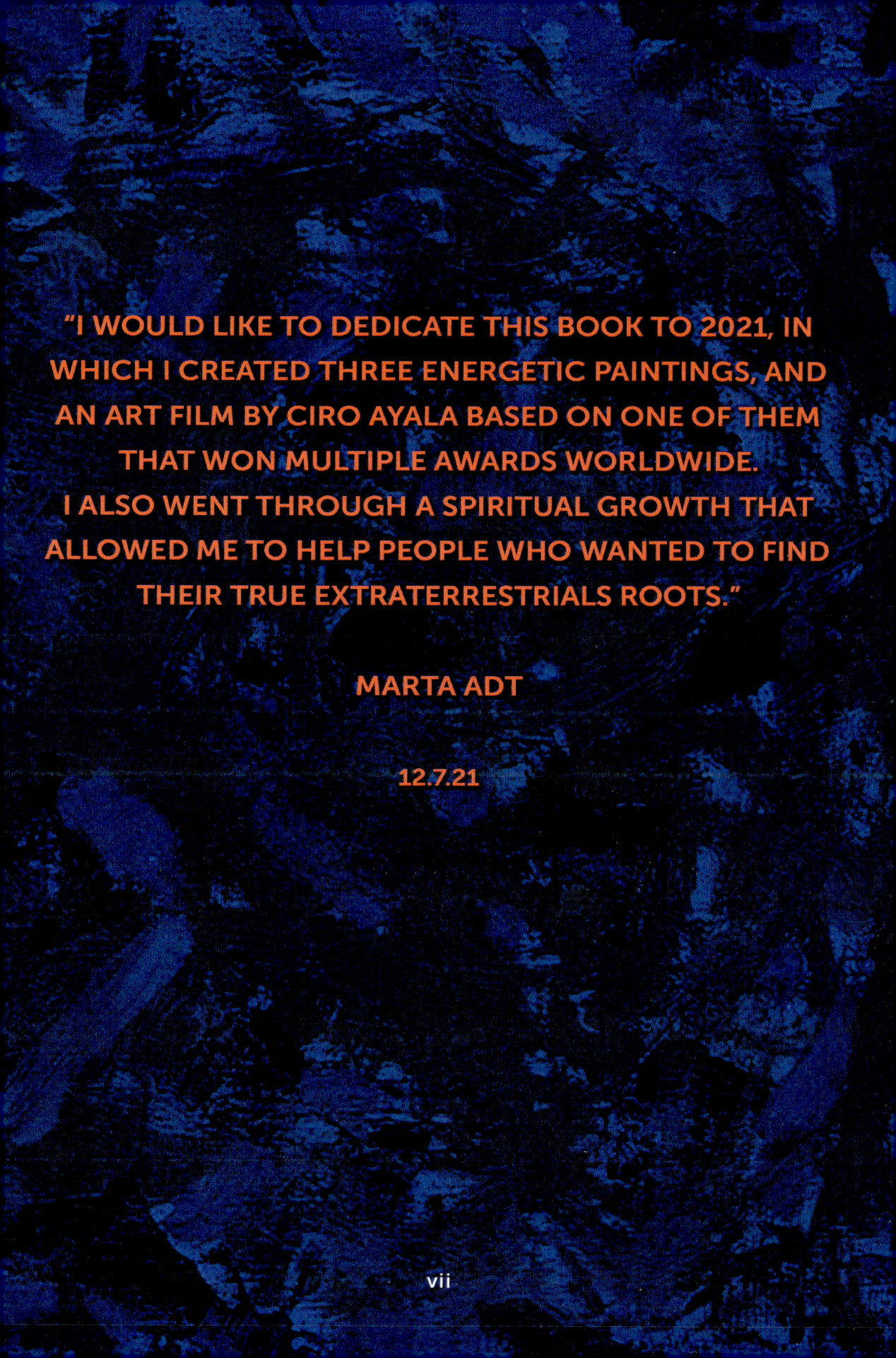

"I WOULD LIKE TO DEDICATE THIS BOOK TO 2021, IN WHICH I CREATED THREE ENERGETIC PAINTINGS, AND AN ART FILM BY CIRO AYALA BASED ON ONE OF THEM THAT WON MULTIPLE AWARDS WORLDWIDE.
I ALSO WENT THROUGH A SPIRITUAL GROWTH THAT ALLOWED ME TO HELP PEOPLE WHO WANTED TO FIND THEIR TRUE EXTRATERRESTRIALS ROOTS."

MARTA ADT

12.7.21

DEAR READER,

ALL EVENTS HAVE A MUCH DEEPER MEANING THAN WE CAN IMAGINE. REALIZING YOUR TRUE DIVINE ORIGIN AND REMEMBERING A PIECE OF THE COSMIC HISTORY OF YOUR SOUL, IT WILL HELP YOU BETTER UNDERSTAND YOUR STRENGTHS, ABILITIES AND, PERHAPS, EVEN OPEN THE VEIL OF YOUR DESTINY, YOU WILL ALSO KNOW WHO (BESIDES YOUR HIGHER SELF, ANGELS, ARCHANGELS AND SPIRITUAL GUIDES) TO TURN TO FOR HELP, HEALING AND GUIDANCE.

MANY CHILDREN OF THE UNIVERSE LACK THE SUPPORT OF THEIR GALACTIC FAMILY… THIS BOOK WILL HELP YOU FIND YOUR TRUE SELF THAT HAS BEEN HIDDEN BY SOCIETY, HISTORY, CULTURE AND TRADITIONS SINCE THE TIME YOU WERE BORN.

ARE YOU READY FOR THE JOURNEY?

MARTA ADT

STAR SEEDS MEETING

© COPYRIGHT MMXXI MARTA ADT - ADT & AYALA ART

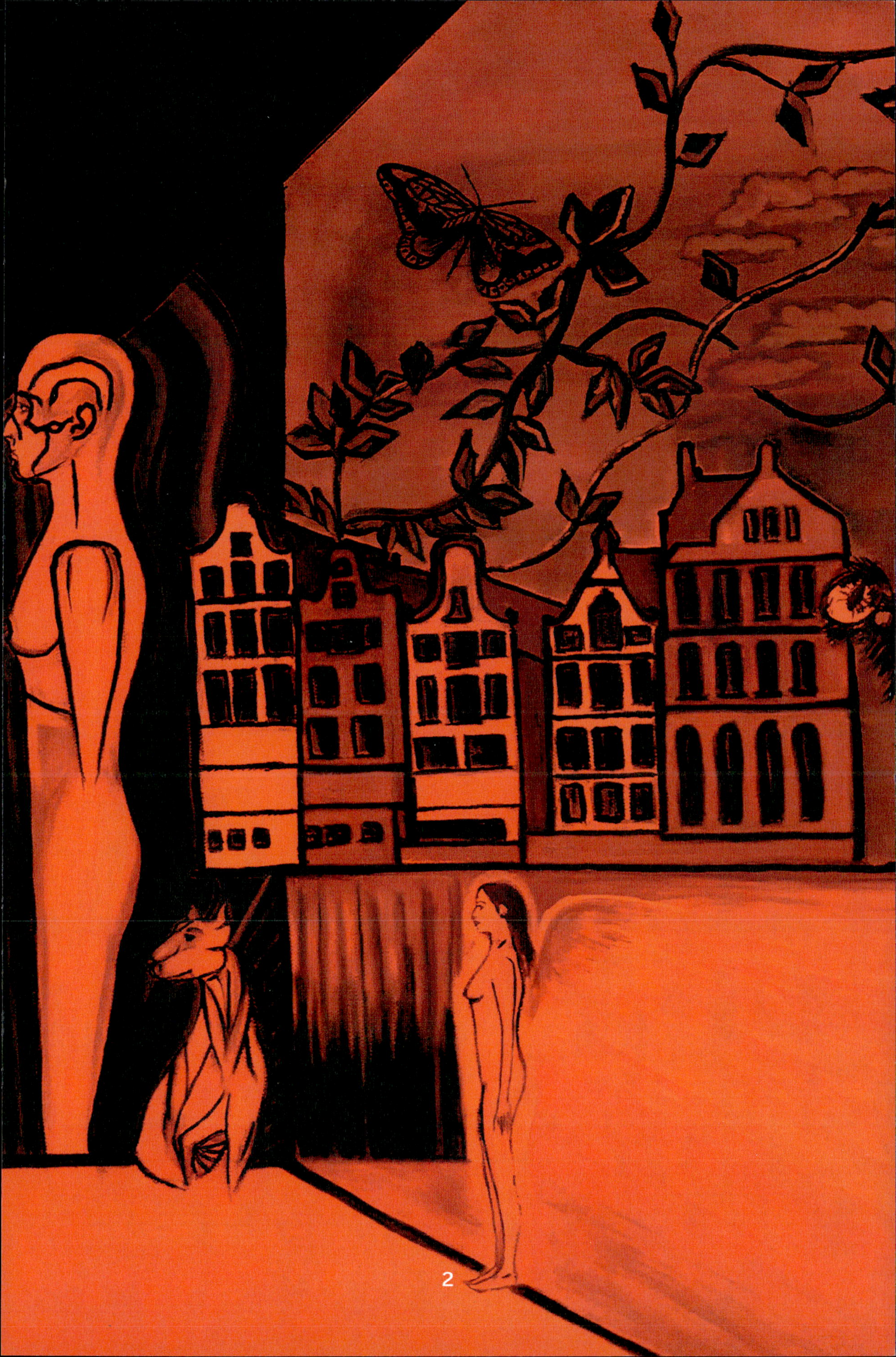

A LITTLE ABOUT ME

I was born in Moscow in 1982, in a family where almost all male lines were creative people...
Since childhood, I have felt different from everyone else.
It took me about 39 years to explore my personality and soul. At the age of 16, I became interested in Philosophy, Buddhism, although I was Orthodox.
At 20, fate began to bring me together with spiritual people. And the higher my spiritual level became, the environment and spiritual teachers changed.
At the age of 30, I was told that I needed to create paintings and transfer my energy to people through art. At that moment, I felt the support of the ADT family and my life changed completely. Views and values have changed, and a profound transformation has taken place. I realized that I had died and a new personality, a new me, was born.
This period lasted about 3 years. It was the most sickly and difficult. There were moments when I didn't want to live, but later I realized that Higher forces had stabbed my spirit and made me strong. After all, we are given only those trials that we can overcome.

And in 2020, on the 25th of December, I found out that I was a Starseed; making me realize the answers to many questions of my life at once.

4

STARSEED AWAKENING

My knowledge of Starseeds began with regression hypnosis, from where I learned that I'm a Starseed and found out my mission on Earth, which is very important for all to know to follow your path.

I started to study Kundalini Reiki, reached the level of Master Teacher and one day in a special astral traveling I went to the place, where my soul was born. I met my soul family and it's impossible to express these feeling of happiness in words. I had tears and didn't want to leave Arcturus.

Now I do this astral traveling for people, who feel that they are not from Earth, who wants to meet their families and ask them questions about their missions, future, past, and maybe to have possibility to meet someone here on Earth.

I have discovered that many humans are Starseeds and come to Earth from different planes and stars. Fate has began to attract such humans to me in order to help them reveal their true origins.

Many already know that representatives of Light Civilizations (and dark ones too), embodied in human bodies, walk among people.

Most of the Starseeds have had their cosmic roots deliberately erased. But now it's time to remember your real selves, to put all aspects together.
All the Starseeds incarnated here for a reason, with a specific mission. And all the conditions from the moment and place of birth to contracts with other souls, were agreed long before your incarnation.
Therefore, do not think that anything in your life happened by accident.

For a Starseed it's rare to be a pure 'breed' of only one Starseed type. Why? Because Starseeds have often lived multiple lives on many different planets, stars, galactic systems and universes.

Most Starseeds are what I call *'hybrid starseeds'*.

CONNECTED SOULS #2

ORIGINAL ARTWORK BY MARTA ADT
SIZE: 100CM X 100CM
OIL ON CANVAS
2021

"THE STORY OF THE PAINTING *CONNECTED SOULS #2* CAME INTUITIVELY WHEN I WAS EXPLORING THE TOPICS OF LOVE, RELATIONSHIPS, KARMA AND FATE. THEY ALL INSPIRED ME TO CREATE THIS PICTURE."

MARTA ADT

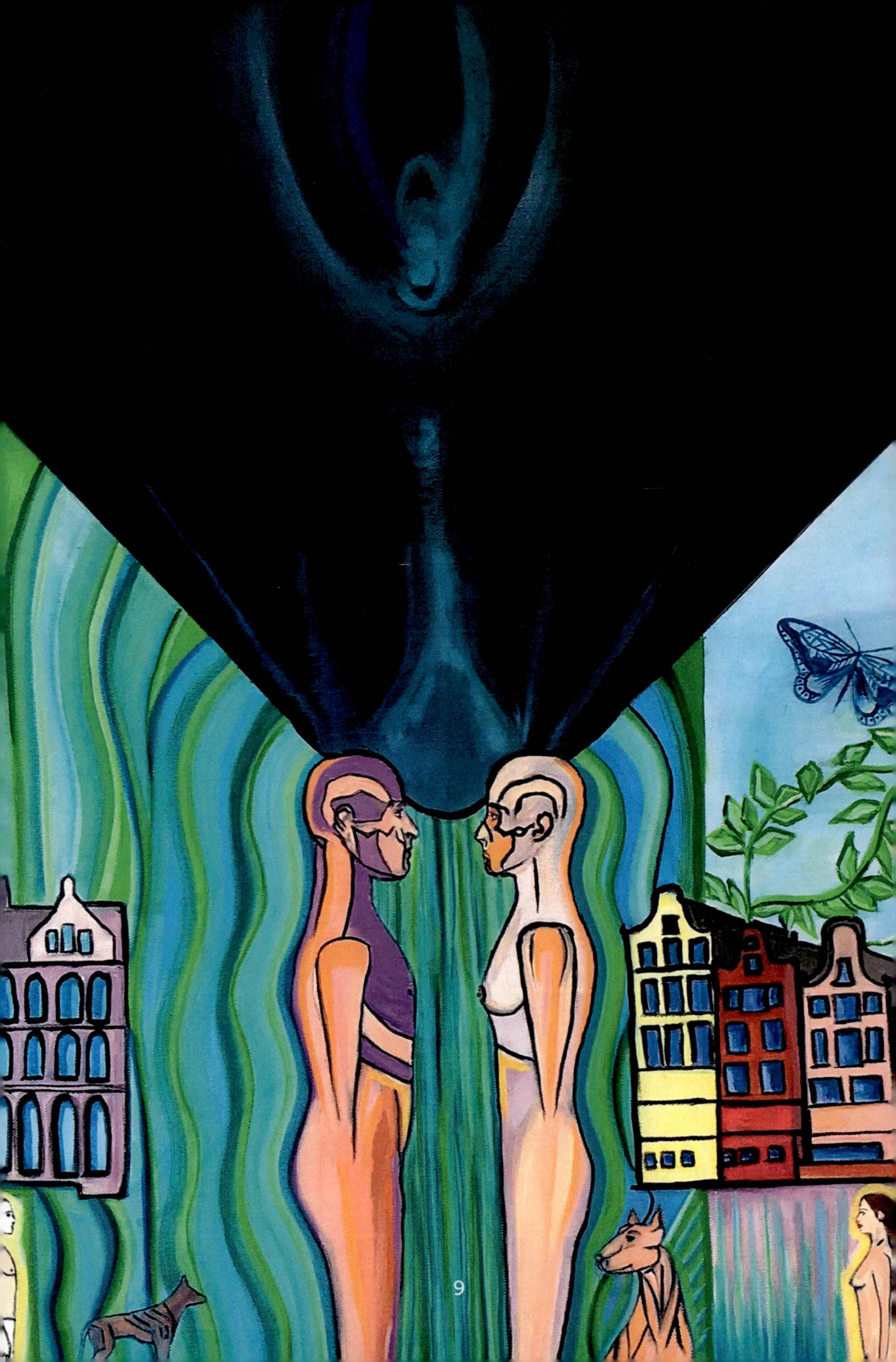

STARSEEDS CHARACTERISTICS

Starseeds are different -not only spiritually but also physically- from normal earthlings.
Starseeds are old and wise souls, and their eyes depict that. They have eyes of the keen observer who can even see the minute details.
As they are highly intelligent, their eyes show wisdom. Usually, they have large and magnetic eyes; but some could have small eyes as well having different shapes and colors.
But one thing is for sure when you look in their eyes, you see curiosity and depth as they know the unknown.

Starseeds physical symptoms could instantly help you to know if you are one. It is not necessary that all the traits are present in the person, but having most of them will help.

SENSITIVITY TOWARDS EXTREME TEMPERATURES
Starseeds are either highly sensitive to hot or cold. The ones, who like warmer weather, find it hard in the cold. On the other hand, cold tolerating Starseed are not comfortable in the hot weather. Their sensitivities are present by birth and will continue until the end.

SENSITIVITY TOWARDS PAIN

Here again, they are the extremists; either they can tolerate intense pain, or they can't even bear a pinprick. Once they become sensitive, it will remain with them forever.

STURDY BODY AND STRONG IMMUNITY

Which body type they have doesn't matter. They are always strong from inside. The healing power of their bodies is also very fast. It heals injuries and strains in no time.
They usually have strong immune systems that keep them safe. Although, there's very little chance of them countering any disease; but when they do, they recover fast. It is because of their origin

UNKNOWN BRUISES ON BODY

Many Starseeds get bruised quite easily. They are unable to recall where they got them. These marks are usually prominent enough to be noticed by others as well.

STRANGE BIRTHMARKS

Starseeds are usually born with strange birthmarks. They also have distinctive moles on the body. The appearance of their birthmark is of special design or shape that might seem unfamiliar and out of this world.

NATURE LOVER

Animals and plants make them feel more comfortable than their fellow human beings. They like to spend time with nature. Starseeds are not fond of artificial lights and find peace and coziness in the sunlight only. Animals also seem attracted to them by feeling comfort and calmness.

ABOVE-AVERAGE HEARING

Their hearing power is better than the average person. As they can sense more, loud sounds can disturb them easily. Now and then, they can hear high-pitched sounds in one or both ears. When the soul is ascending, it becomes a common occurrence. These sounds are present with tingling sensations and increased head pressure. However, these conditions don't last long and they go away within a few days or weeks.

SENSITIVITY TOWARDS ALCOHOL AND MEDICINE

Starseeds have the tendency to be highly sensitive towards drugs, alcohol, and different types of medicine. Some cannot bear it, while others have a high tolerance.

AS THERE'S A GREAT CHANCE OF GOING TOWARDS SUBSTANCE ABUSE, STARSEEDS SHOULD AVOID THE USE OF THESE THINGS -IN THE FIRST PLACE- BECAUSE THEY ONLY KEEP THEM AWAY FROM REALITY AND KNOWING THEIR TRUE LIFE PURPOSE.

BEING NIGHT OWLS

Starseeds feel good and find peace at night; they are night owls and stay up at night more than others.

When Starseeds sleep early at night, something wakes them up in the middle of the night for no reason, especially around 3 am.

Their sleeping patterns are not like other humans. They can go about their day with less sleep than the average person. However, there are times when they need more sleep because of extreme exhaustion; it is also necessary for their spiritual growth.

MARS&VENUS

ORIGINAL ARTWORK BY MARTA ADT

SIZE: 80CM X 50CM

OIL ON CANVAS

2021

(THE PAINTING WAS COMPLETED IN 2021 DURING THE MARS AND VENUS PLANETARY CONJUNCTION.)

"THIS ABSTRACT PAINTING REFLECTS ON THE THEME OF UNITY BETWEEN OPPOSITES: MALE AND FEMALE, BODY AND MIND, WAR AND PEACE, CHAOS AND ORDER... A POWERFUL ALLIANCE THAT TRANSCENDS TIME AND SPACE."

MARTA ADT

PLEIADIAN STARSEEDS

Pleiadians come from Pleiades, a beautiful star cluster known as the Seven Sisters and Messier 45 in the Taurus constellation.

PURPOSE

According to Western Hermeticism, Pleiadians are considered the record keepers of the Earth. They are known to be highly knowledgeable and have advanced healing abilities.

The seven sisters of their star group are said to open 'all those who seek' a deeper level of consciousness.

It's said that Pleiades is a "school of learning", where beings from all corners of the universe can reincarnate to develop their understanding of the essence of nature.

Pleiadians are here to help the human race evolve, ready for the Golden Age transformation.

It is said that Pleiadians naturally exist in the fifth dimension, the birthplace of love and creativity.

As a result, these beings are advanced in the arts as well as traditional healing practices such as Reiki, crystal healing, and counselling.

PLEIADIAN STARSEED TRAITS

- Can feel 'wise and mature' as an Earth being.
- True humanitarians.
- Strongly empathic.
- Feel like they have a big mission on Earth.
- Family-oriented. Very good with children and animals.
- May exhibit strong feminine, nurturing energy.
- Gentle in nature.
- Averse to harm and violence.
- Perfectionists.
- People-pleasers, often to their own detriment.
- Very polite, soft spoken.
- Very drawn to astrology, spirituality, meta-physics, space, astronomy.
- Skilled healers, extremely gifted in arts, creative fields and counselling.
- Spreads love easily. Wishes everyone else was just as loving.
- Can be highly sensitive people.
- May have Northern European or Norse heritage.
- Understands balance: yin/yang, light/dark, sun/moon.
- Might suffer with anxiety, depression and self-esteem issues when not in alignment with their true nature.

SIRIAN STARSEEDS

These beautiful souls come from the stars Sirius A and Sirius B, with the latter being the brightest star in Earth' sky. Sirius B vibrates at an incredibly high, non-physical, 6D frequency.
It is widely believed that these two stars gave rise to the awakening of humans.

PURPOSE
Sirians are the peacekeepers and guardians of the world. Their sole aim is to watch over our evolution and guide us during times of turbulence.
Their secondary mission involves bringing divine harmony, love and peace to all those who walk this Earth.

SIRIAN STARSEED TRAITS
- Drawn to the Sirius star system.
- Lead a simple, but spiritual life.
- Very open minded.
- Struggle to express personal feelings.
- "Gaia's people": very drawn to caring for our Earth during evolution.
- Very loyal as friends.

- Maintain a tight-knit circle of friends.
- Fantastic sense of humor and not afraid to act silly.
- Feel like they have a mission to save animals or nature.
- Drawn to lost civilizations, myths and legends.
- Calm and adjusted.
- Intense daydreamers.
- May be attracted to the ocean and water if from Sirius B.
- Have a difficult time expressing emotions in their relationships.

Arcturians are very intelligent beings; they are the critical thinkers by birth and appear like leaders. Their nature is quiet and they don't open up to others easily. Anger is their primary emotion known. As other Starseeds, they also have particular work on the Earth. They are the builders and planners of a new society. Their innovative nature not only helps in structuring but also building proper systems that benefit humans.

Arcturians are natural born leaders with very strong personalities, and they form part of the most advanced civilization in our known universe.

PURPOSE

Arcturians are mainly physicists, architects, community planners, mathematicians, system designers, musicians, and geometry artists. They want to experiment new things and implement their ideas.

The Arcturians want the humans to enter the fourth and fifth dimensions, and also teach them to raise their frequencies of vibrations.

They are known to be the protectors and guardians of the higher consciousness not only on earth but in the whole universe.

ARCTURIAN STARSEED TRAITS

- Drawn to Arcturus star system.
- Natural born leaders.
- Very charismatic.
- Incredibly telepathic.
- Highly passionate about their work.
- Great public speakers.
- Love attention, extroverted.
- May seem big-headed or egotistical if out of alignment.
- Highly intelligent and motivated.
- Tendency to rise to the top.
- Often found in fields such as: mathematics, data, science, communication, technology, medicine, engineering, architecture…
- Interested in how things work.
- Can be compassionate, but very guarded with their emotions.
- May seem callous as they're not in tune with other people's emotions.
- Gifted at the art of divination/tarot.
- Good channelers.
- Interested in the mathematical side of spirituality e.g. sacred geometry, natal charts (signs, degrees etc).
- Often very confident, with a high drive for success.
- Wants to live in a world where spirituality and science can blend.
- Show anger when they're upset.

LYRAN STARSEEDS

Lyra is the small constellation with the bright star Vega. Lyrans incarnated in other star systems as well, including our solar system.

Lyrans were the first ones to seed our universe. They are said to be associated with the feline body; even in the human form, they have cat-like eyes and nose. Lyrans are known for their knowledge in genetics. They are the root race of human beings and made the human genes. They also taught Atlantic and Lemuria about physical energy and its use. Using their vast knowledge, they have created many machines and devices that improved the lives of humans.

Lyran Starseeds are travellers. They love to know the world. Physical activity is also their thing, and they are mostly athletes and perfect in their fields. Their survival skills are also unmatchable.
Their intuition is also quite accurate, and they can easily rely on it. They are the walking lie detectors and can easily differentiate between the fake and the real.

When they know how to work with their energy, they are confident; but when they don't, they become highly self-conscious.
They can be impatient, jealous and moody at times.

Constant change makes them happy and they don't want to remain in the same place for a long time.

VEGA STARSEEDS

Vega starseeds or vegans come from the constellation of Lyra to inhabit the brightest star in our sky: Sirius.

They were the first species to develop space travel and colonize other star systems.

There are groups of Vegan starseeds who came from other constellations such as Ursa Major, Pleiades, and Arcturus.

In the Sirius star system, these beings were known to have blue skin due to their suns radiance. They are known as the "blue race".

They are known to be highly artistic beings and some of them have occupied other planets in the universe.

PURPOSE

Their mission is to help humanity evolve towards spiritual illumination.

They are strongly committed to human progression, especially within the realms of human intelligence, awareness, and spirituality.

Their minds are not limited by human theories, which makes them compassionate observers who love to see things from a different point of view.

VEGA STARSEED TRAITS

- They are very creative in terms of technology and design.
- Have the ability to see energy or chakras, most of them are energy healers and have strong psychic abilities.
- They are very attractive and beautiful souls with vivid imaginations, creative flair, and acute sensitivity.
- They are also known to be very kind souls with strong psychic abilities.
- Their skin is usually light blue or lavender in color, often with white or silver hair.
- Vegans are spiritually intense. When it comes to spirituality Vegans use mostly their feminine energy.
- They are more sensitive, empathetic, caring, and compassionate.
- They have a strong sense of justice and fair play.
- They have a vivid imagination and an open mind about everything new, which makes them highly creative beings.
- They always want to explore and learn new things in life which makes them knowledgeable beings.
- Vega starseeds have a prominent heart chakra that is very big and open all the time.
- They are highly empathetic.
- They're very easy to be around, approachable, and loved by many because of their magnetic personalities.

ORION STARSEEDS

Orion starseeds are a fascinating type of starseed, hailing from the gorgeous Orion constellation. Drawn to ancient wisdom, knowledge and logic, these starseeds are the truth seekers amongst us.

Orion starseeds come from one of the most famous constellations in Earth's sky: Orion. It's one of the brightest and most recognizable forms in the night sky, and can be seen throughout the world.

PURPOSE

Their purpose on Earth is to help improve our civilization's knowledge in fields such as science, technology and medicine.

Their personal, spiritual mission is to open their heart centre, and learn to be more trusting.

ORION STARSEED TRAITS

- Drawn to Orion constellation
- Compassionate activists about things they're interested in doing.
- Task-oriented and love their work.
- Most likely to be entrepreneurs.
- Dream of inspiring and leading others.
- True knowledge seekers.
- Love to learn.

- "Jack of all trades" — have a lot of knowledge about lots of topics.
- Often incarnate as Earth signs: Virgo, Taurus, Capricorn.
- Interested in science — biology, chemistry, physics, astronomy.
- Calm and adjusted.
- Very rarely get angry or show outbursts of emotion.
- Unintentionally may come off as cold.
- Hold logic above all else.

Orions have bad races too: Greys -a particular sub-race of Orions- are said to be stuck here reincarnating on Earth life after life. This is due to their karma cycle and their interference with Earth beings in a previous past life.

They are believed to have traumatised and hurt humans which galactically means they're stuck here karmically.

To clarify, Orions aren't a bad Starseed type. They're just different than other Starseeds in the way they think and function.

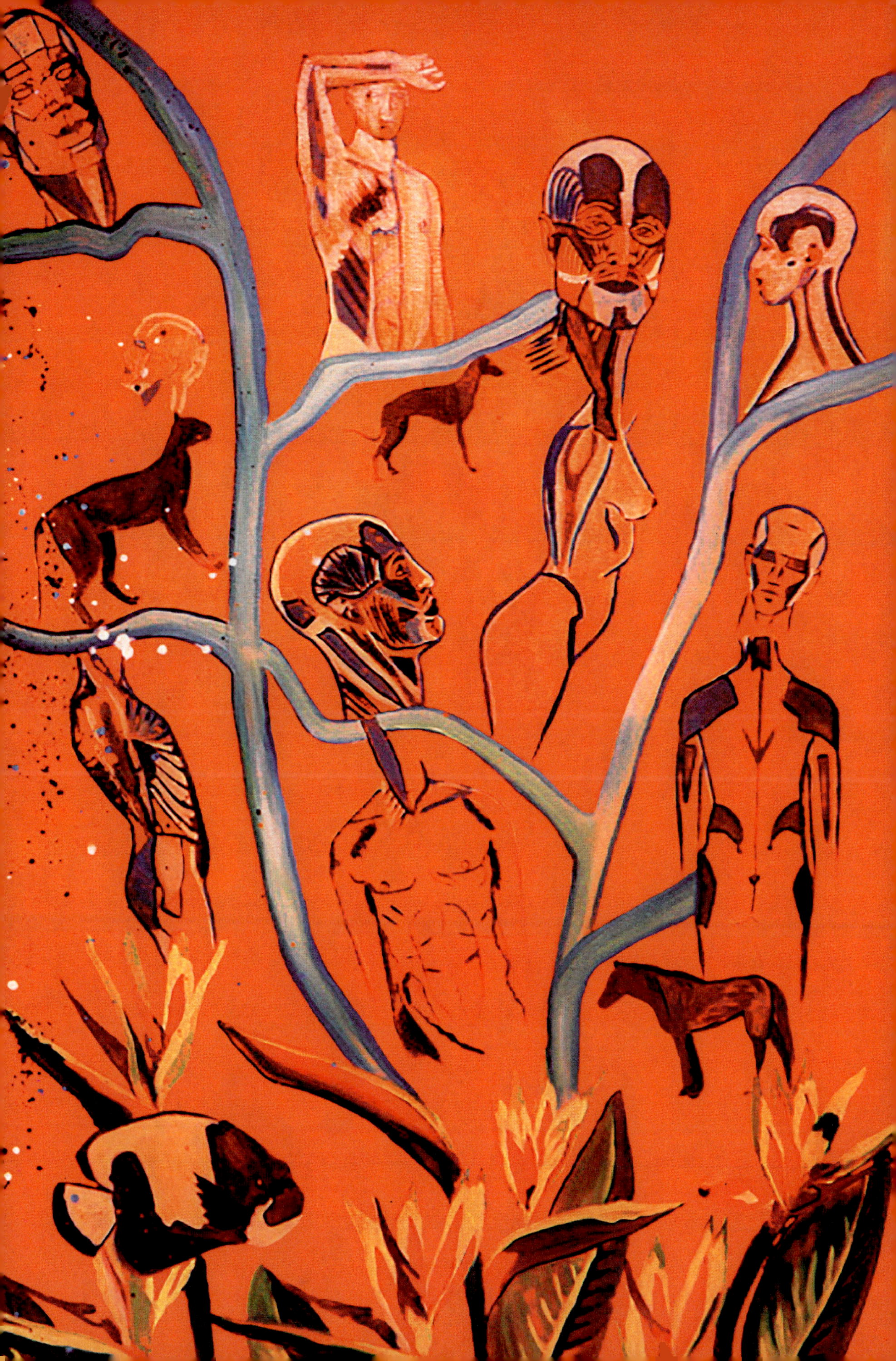

MY ASTRAL TRAVEL SESSIONS

IT ALL STARTS WITH ENTERING IN A MEDITATIVE STATE. YOUR CONSCIOUSNESS SLOWLY BEGINS TO SEPARATE FROM THE BODY, AND IT INCREASES IN SIZE. WITH THE HELP OF CERTAIN ENERGIES, TEACHERS AND MENTORS, YOUR CONSCIOUSNESS THEN GETS TO THE PLACE WHERE YOUR SOUL WAS BORN.

PERSONAL EXPERIENCES

In my astral experience, I got to Arcturus. There I saw my soul family who were very tall people (taller than me).

I was so overwhelmingly happy that I can't describe it in normal words.

During the astral journey, I asked my soul family the questions I was interested in and when it was time to go back, I started crying: I didn't want to leave them.

Nevertheless, my children were waiting for me on Earth so I had to return to continue with my life mission and help those who truly want to know their spiritual roots....

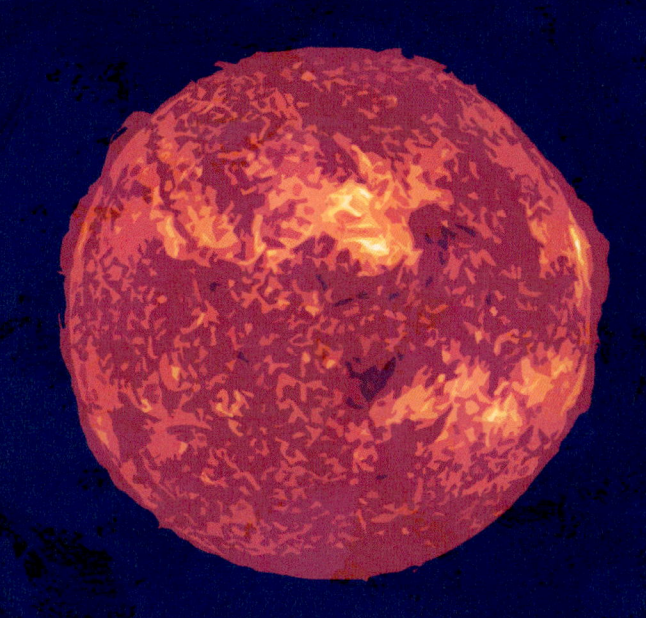

NADIA SHARAPOVA

I am a psychologist living in Moscow, interested in everything related to the human being and the structure of his psyche.

Lately, I have been interested in studying and researching topics about energy, the immaterial and everything that hasn't been investigated deeply in sciences or that is out of reach through normal measure-methodologies.

Marta Adt introduced me to Reiki, and I tried out an astral journey to explore the origins of my existence. This is how I found out that my soul is from the constellation of Orion.

During the session, I was able to ask questions and find answers about my past.
The whole experience has been very interesting for me.

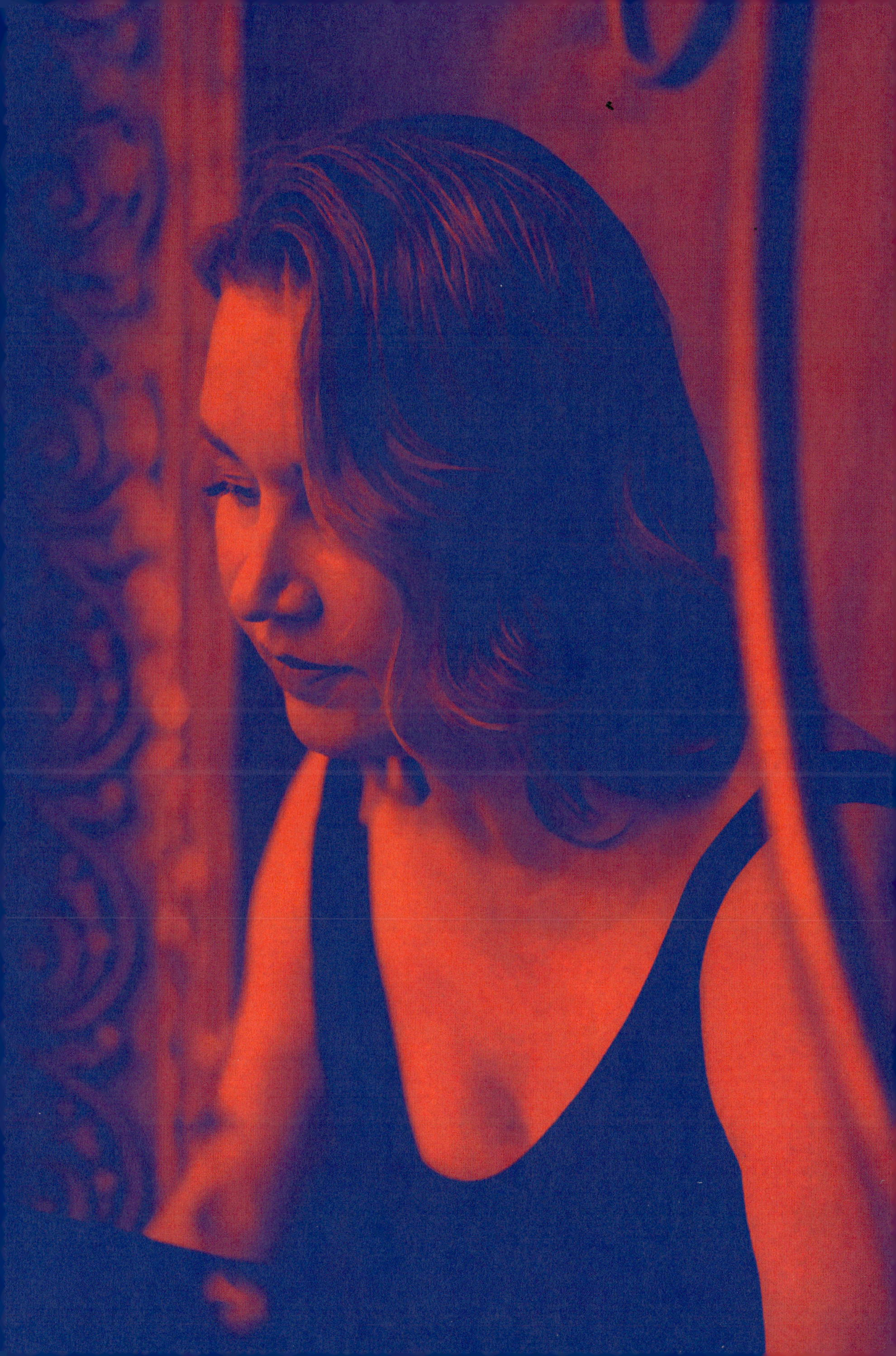

INNA KOLYADA

I'm a movie and theater actress who lives and works in Moscow. I also teach yoga and raise a cute dog.

During a very difficult period of my life, in which I almost did not survive, I met Marta Adt who began to help me heal and overcome obstacles by the use of Reiki.
At one of the astral travel meditations, I found out that I am a star soul from "Nebula Nebula". There I saw my spiritual family, who answered me many questions.
They revealed the reasons for my mistakes, and what exactly I am doing wrong.
It was a very warm and comfortable experience. I felt that I was finally acknowledging the importan things in my life and existence.
I felt real support and help through these distant galaxies...

I now look at the world in a completely different way and I started evaluating circumstances and people's actions based on a different point of view and logic.
I've become more confident and peaceful. It's like there's always support from within myself.

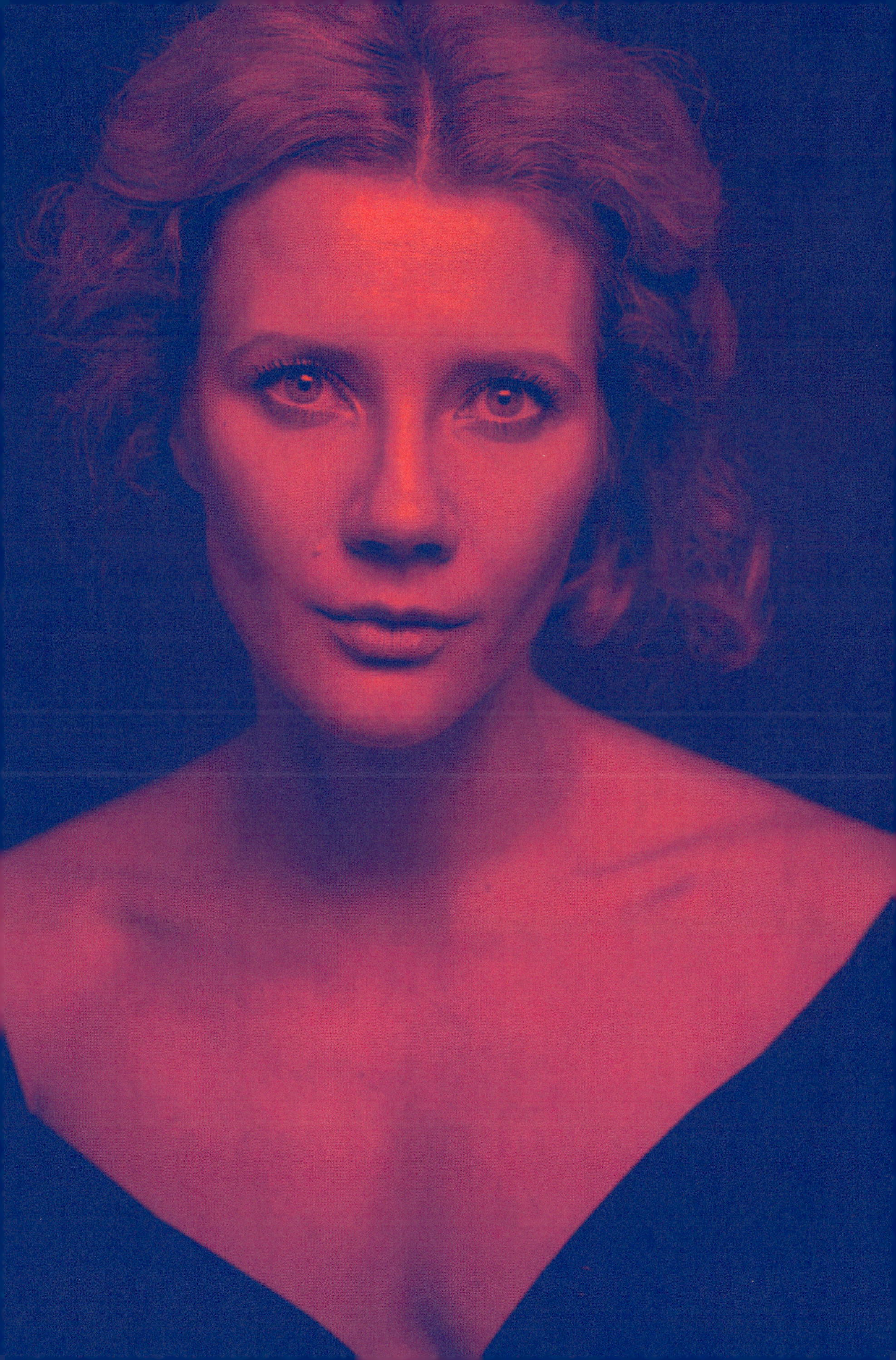

TONAL/NAGUAL

ORIGINAL ARTWORK BY MARTA ADT

SIZE: 100CM X 120CM

OIL ON CANVAS

2021

"THE PAINTING DESCRIBES THE LINK BETWEEN THE PARALLEL WORLDS OF FINITE MATERIAL OBJECTS (THE TONAL) AND THE NON-MATERIAL INFINITE REALM (THE NAGUAL), CONSTANTLY INTERTWINED IN MAGICAL BEAUTY."

MARTA ADT

FINAL WORDS

REMEMBER: YOU SHOULD DEDICATE YOURSELF TO DISCOVER YOUR ORIGINS AND YOUR SOUL MISSION, THEN USE THAT SENSE OF PURPOSE AND DETERMINATION TO HELP ELEVATE HUMANITY AS WE ENTER THIS MORE CONNECTED, ENLIGHTENED, AND UNITED ERA.

SO, STAR TRAVELERS, ARE YOU READY TO KNOW YOUR EXTRATERRESTRIAL ROOTS?

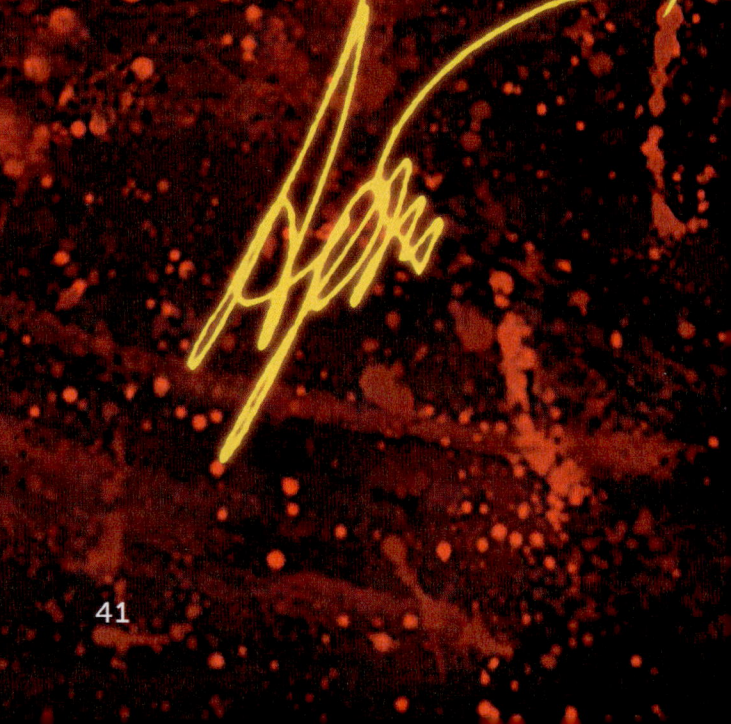

NOT
"THE END"
BUT
"THE BEGINNING OF
YOUR AWAKENING"

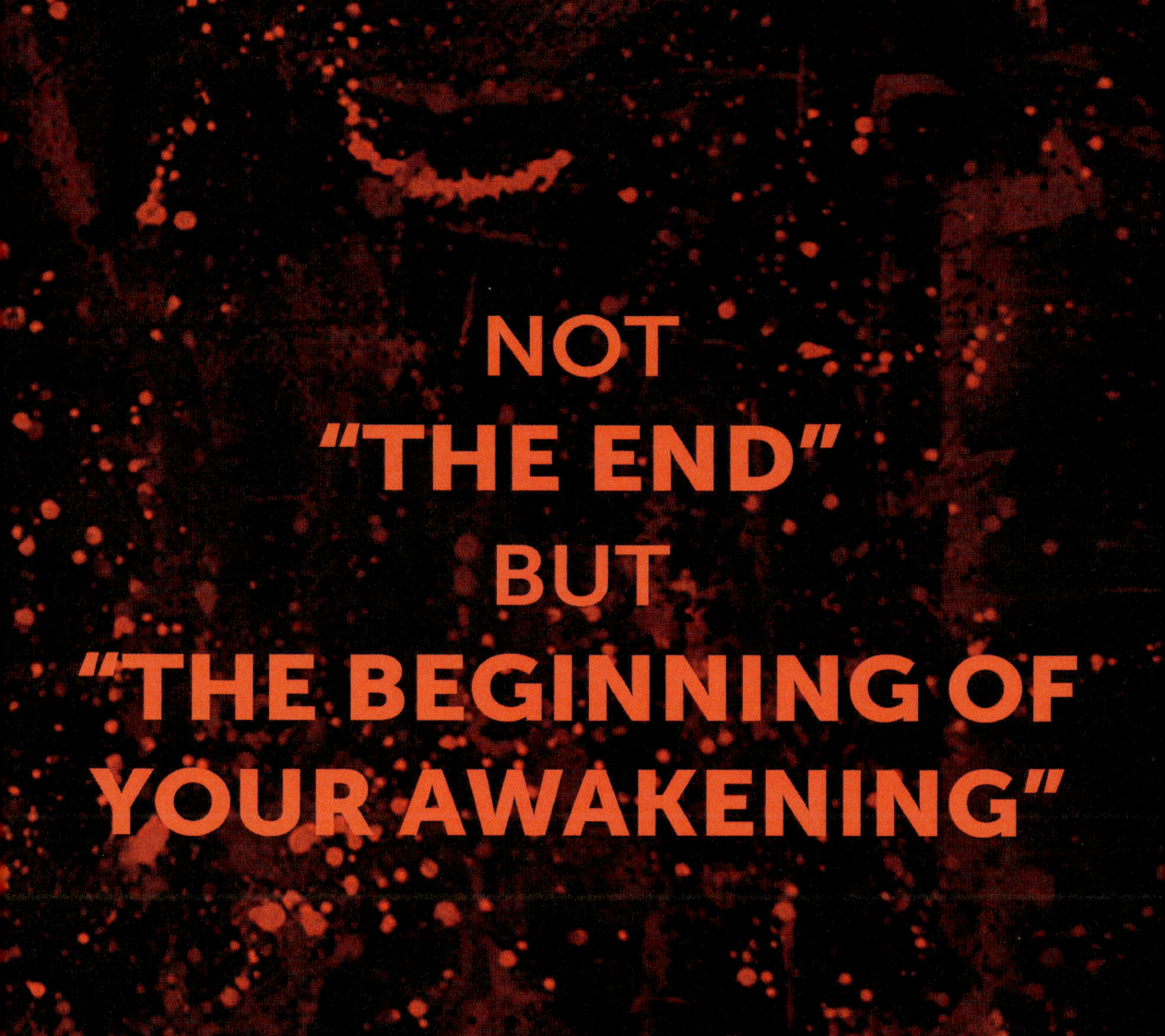

SPECIAL THANKS TO:
MY ANCESTORS,
MY TEACHERS,
MENTORS,
ANGELS
& ARCHANGELS.

IF YOU WANT TO LEARN MORE
ABOUT ASTRAL TRAVEL AND STARSEEDS,
DON'T HESITATE TO CONTACT ME AT:

FB: @alphareikimaster

IG: @alpha.reiki

Email: alphareikimaster@gmail.com

www.alphareiki.life